NANA'S BOOKS
Engagement + Nostalgia = Joy

YONDER COME DAY

Yonder come day, day is breaking
Yonder come day, oh my soul
Yonder come day, day is breaking
Sun is rising in my soul

Yonder, Yonder.
Yonder, Yonder.
Sun is rising in my soul

Trees are green and the air is sweet.
The good earth is singin' underneath my feet.
I point my feet down that freedom line.
Walking that road, I'm feeling fine.

Traditional Georgia Sea Islands Gullah Spiritual
Carlotta Mae Corpron, *Delores, Melrose Plantation, Louisiana*, 1948
Amon Carter Museum of American Art Archives, Fort Worth, Texas

OVER JORDAN

O come and go with me,
If from sin you would be free;
You will find it good for thee,
Over Jordan.
'Tis a land of corn and wine,
And there's fruit of every kind;
You will find it is sublime,
Over Jordan.
Over Jordan, over Jordan,
O it is a pleasant place,
For I have the "second grace."
Over Jordan's rolling sand
Into happy Beulah land,
'Tis a pleasant place to live,
Over Jordan.
Many will not enter in,
For they want to cling to sin,
And their journey won't begin,
Over Jordan.
And they see the giants there,
For their vision is not clear,
And they will not go for fear,
Over Jordan.

Traditional Hymn
Edward Lamson Henry, *Protecting the Groceries*, 1886
Private Collection

ALL THROUGH THE NIGHT

Sleep my child and peace attend thee,
All through the night;
Guardian angels God will send thee,
All through the night.
Soft the drowsy hours are creeping,
Hill and vale in slumber sleeping
I my loving vigil keeping,
All through the night.
While the moon her watch is keeping
All through the night;
While the weary world is sleeping,
All through the night.
Over thy spirit gently stealing,
Visions of delight revealing,
Breathes a pure and holy feeling,
All through the night.
Star of Faith the dark adorning,
All through the night
Leads us fearless towards the morning,
All through the night
Though our hearts be wrapped in sorrow,
From the home of dawn we borrow,
Promise of a glad tomorrow,
All through the night.

Howard E. Boulton, c.1844
Sargent Claude Johnson, Mother and Child, *c.1932*
San Francisco Museum of Modern Art

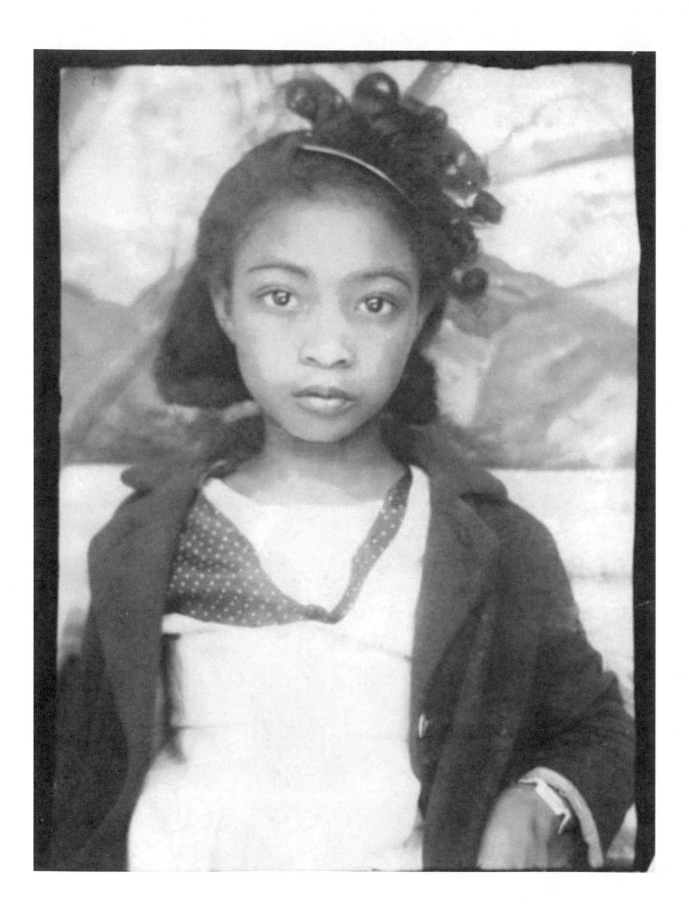

NOBODY KNOWS THE TROUBLE I'VE SEEN

Nobody knows the trouble I've seen
Nobody knows but Jesus
Nobody knows the trouble I've seen
Glory, Hallelujah
Sometimes I'm up, sometimes
I'm down, oh, yes Lord
Sometimes I'm almost
To the ground, oh yes, Lord
Nobody knows the trouble I've seen
Nobody knows but Jesus
Anybody knows the trouble I've seen
Glory, Hallelujah
If you got there before I do, oh yes Lord
Tell all my friends,
I'm coming too, oh yes Lord
Nobody knows the trouble I've seen
Nobody knows but Jesus
Nobody knows the trouble I've seen
Glory, Hallelujah

Traditional Spiritual
Photographer Unknown
Private Collection

HOW GREAT THOU ART

When through the woods, and forest glades I wander,
And hear the birds sing sweetly in the trees.
When I look down, from lofty mountain grandeur
And see the brook, and feel the gentle breeze.

Then sings my soul, My Saviour God, to Thee,
How great Thou art, How great Thou art.
Then sings my soul, My Saviour God, to Thee,
How great Thou art, How great Thou art!

And when I think, that God, His Son not sparing;
Sent Him to die, I scarce can take it in;
That on a Cross, my burdens gladly bearing,
He bled and died to take away my sin.

Then sings my soul, My Saviour God, to Thee,
How great Thou art, How great Thou art.
Then sings my soul, My Saviour God, to Thee,
How great Thou art, How great Thou art!

Carl Gustav Boberg, 1885
Joseph Judd Pennell, *Portrait of Roger Hammond Children*, 1923
Private Collection

SWING LOW SWEET CHARIOT

Swing low, sweet chariot,
coming for to carry me home;
swing low, sweet chariot,
coming for to carry me home.

I looked over Jordan, and what did I see,
coming for to carry me home?
A band of angels coming after me,
coming for to carry me home.

If you get there before I do,
coming for to carry me home;
tell all my friends I'm coming too,
coming for to carry me home.

I'm sometimes up, I'm sometimes down,
coming for to carry me home;
but still my soul feels heavenly bound,
coming for to carry me home.

Traditional Spiritual
Henry Ossawa Tanner, The *Banjo Lesson*, 1866
Hampton University, Hampton, Virginia

PRECIOUS LORD, TAKE MY HAND

Precious Lord, take my hand,
Lead me on, let me stand
I'm tired, I'm weak, I'm lone
Through the storm, through the night
Lead me on to the light
Take my hand precious Lord, lead me home

When my way grows drear, precious Lord, linger near
When my light is almost gone
Hear my cry, hear my call
Hold my hand lest I fall
Take my hand precious Lord, lead me home

When the darkness appears and the night draws near
And the day is past and gone
At the river I stand
Guide my feet, hold my hand
Take my hand precious Lord, lead me home

Precious Lord, take my hand
Lead me on, let me stand
I'm tired, I'm weak, I'm lone
Through the storm, through the night
Lead me on to the light
Take my hand precious Lord, lead me home

Thomas Andew Dorsey, after George N. Allen, 1855
Winold Reiss, *Father and Two Children, St. Helena (1886-1953)*
Alfred Steiglitz Collection, Fisk University, Nashville, Tennessee

PEACE IN THE VALLEY

I am tired and weary but I must toil on
'Til the Lord comes to call me away
Where the morning is bright
And the Lamb is the light
And the night is as fair as the day

There'll be peace in the valley for me, some day
There'll be peace in the valley for me
I pray no more sorrow and sadness or trouble will be
There'll be peace in the valley for me

There the flow'rs will be blooming, the grass will be green
And the skies will be clear and serene
The sun ever shines, giving one endless beam
And no clouds there will ever be seen

There the bear will be gentle, the wolf will be tame
And the lion will lay down by the lamb
The host from the wild will be led by a Child
And I'll be changed from the creature I am

No headaches or heartaches or misunderstands,
No confusion or trouble won't be
No frowns to defile, just a big endless smile,
There'll be peace and contentment for me

Thomas Andrew Dorsey, 1937
Lewis Wickes Hine, *African American Boy Holding a Piece of Fruit, c.1930*
Library of Congress

WILL THERE BE ANY STARS IN MY CROWN

I am thinking today of that beautiful land
I shall reach when the sun goeth down;
When thru wonderful grace by my Savior I stand,
Will there be any stars in my crown

Will there be any stars, any stars in my crown
When at evening the sun goeth down
When I wake with the blest in the mansions of rest,
Will there be any stars in my crown

In the strength of the Lord let me labor and pray,
Let me watch as a winner of souls;
That bright stars may be mine in the glorious day,
When His praise like the sea billow rolls.

Oh, what joy it will be when His face I behold,
Living gems at His feet to lay down;
It would sweeten my bliss in the city of gold,
Should there be any stars in my crown.

E.E. Hewitt, 1897
Simon Maris, *Isabella*, c.1906
Rijksmuseum, Netherlands

GOSPEL TRAIN

All aboard for the gospel train,
My seat's reserved and my ticket's paid.
Gonna be there when the conductor says
All aboard for the gospel train.
All aboard for the gospel train.
Everybody waitin' for the judgment day
When the saints are lifted on the gospel train
There won't be any stopping,
Any waitin' in line,
It's just a one way ticket into paradise.
I'm gonna be waitin' with my bags all packed
When I hear that whistle and a rumblin' tracks.
It's gonna be exciting
When it's ready to go
When I board that train it's gonna take me back home.
All aboard for the gospel train,
 My seat's reserved and my ticket's paid.
Gonna be there when the conductor says
All aboard for the gospel train.
All aboard for the gospel train.
Gonna leave my trials
And my troubles behind,
There's gonna be no sorrow
At the end of the line
Headin' for the city
With the streets of pure gold.

John Chamberlain, 1863
Artist Unknown, *American Beauty*, 1905

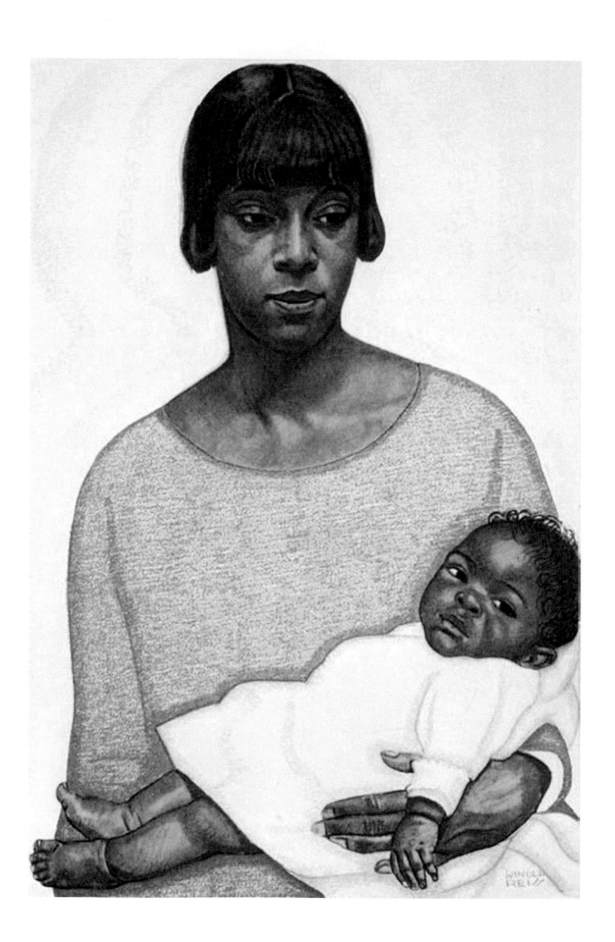

I DON'T FEEL NO WAYS TIRED

I've come too far from where I started from
Nobody told me that the road would be easy
I don't believe He brought me this far to leave me
I don't believe He brought me this far
Nobody told me
Nobody promised me
That the road was gonna be easy

Oh, but I don't believe He brought me this far

Can I get a witness here tonight
I don't know bout you tonight
But I'm been running for Jesus a long time
And there's something about walking with Him, Hallelujah
Every day gets sweeter
Than the day before
And for some reason
I don't mind the pitfalls
Cause every time I get to one,
He's right there
And I can say just like that old mother says that night

I don t feel no ways tired, Lord I've come too far
From where I started from
Nobody told me that the road would be easy
Well I don't believe He'd bring me this far,
And just leave me

Traditional Spiritual
Winold Reiss, *The Brown Madonna*, c. 1925
Fisk University, Catalog of American Portraits, The National Portrait Gallery,
Smithsonian Institution

MANSION OVER THE HILLTOP

If it were not true, I would have told you so
He has gone away to live in that bright city
He's preparing me a mansion up there,
I know I'm satisfied with just a cottage below
A little silver and a little gold
In that bright city where the ransomed will shine
I want a gold one that's silver lined

I've got a mansion just over the hilltop
In that bright land where we'll never grow old

And someday yonder we will never more wander
But walk the streets that are purest gold
Don't think me poor or deserted or lonely
I'm not discouraged, I'm heaven bound
I'm just a pilgrim in search of a city
I want a mansion, a harp and a crown

I've got a mansion just over the hilltop
In that bright land where we'll never grow old
And someday yonder we will never more wander
But walk the streets that are purest gold

Ira F. Stanphill, 1949
William Bullard, *Portrait of Ralph Mendis On a Stoop, c.1902*
Worcester Art Museum, Frank Morrill Archive

THE LILY OF THE VALLEY

I've found a friend in Jesus, He's everything to me,
He's the fairest of ten thousand to my soul;
The Lily of the Valley, in Him alone I see
All I need to cleanse and make me fully whole.
In sorrow He's my comfort, in trouble, He's my stay;
He tells me every care on Him to roll.

He's the Lily of the Valley, the Bright and Morning Star,
He's the fairest of ten thousand to my soul.
He all my grief has taken, and all my sorrows borne;
In temptation, He's my strong and mighty tow'r;
I've all for Him forsaken, and all my idols torn
From my heart and now He keeps me by His pow'r.
Though all the world forsake me, and Satan tempt me sore,
Through Jesus I shall safely reach the goal.
He'll never, never leave me, nor yet forsake me here,
While I live by faith and do His blessed will;
A wall of fire about me, I've nothing now to fear,
From His manna, He my hungry soul shall fill.
Then sweeping up to glory to see His blessed face,
Where rivers of delight shall ever roll.

Charles W. Fry, 1881
Photographer Unknown

THE STORM IS PASSING OVER

Courage, my soul, and let us journey on,
Tho' the night is dark, it won't be very long.
Thanks be to God, the morning light appears,
And the storm is passing over,

Hallelujah Hallelujah Hallelujah

The storm is passing over, Hallelujah

Billows rolling high, and thunder shakes the ground,
Lightning's flash and tempest all around,
Jesus walks the sea and calms the angry waves,
And the storm is passing over, Hallelujah

The stars have disappeared, and distant lights are dim,
My soul is filled with fears, the seas are breaking in.
I hear the Master cry, Be not afraid, 'tis I,
And the storm will soon be over, Hallelujah

Soon we shall reach the distant shining shore,
Free from all the storms we'll rest forevermore.
Safe within the veil, we'll furl the riven sail,
And the storms will all be over, Hallelujah

Charles Albert Tindley, 1905
William Henry Johnson, *Li'L Sis*, 1944
Smithsonian American Art Museum,
Gift of the Harmon Foundation

IT IS WELL WITH MY SOUL

When peace like a river, attendeth my way,
When sorrows like sea billows roll
Whatever my lot, thou hast taught me to say
It is well, it is well, with my soul

Though Satan should buffet, though trials should
come, Let this blest assurance control,
That Christ has regarded my helpless estate,
And hath shed His own blood for my soul
It is well, it is well
With my soul, with my soul
It is well, it is well with my soul

My sin, oh, the bliss of this glorious thought
My sin, not in part but the whole,
  Is nailed to the cross, and I bear it no more,
Praise the Lord, praise the Lord, O my soul
It is well, it is well
With my soul, with my soul
It is well, it is well with my soul

Horatio G. Spafford, 1873
Mathilde de Cordoba, *Young Boy Drawing* c.1935-1943
Schomberg Center for Research in Black Culture, New York, NY

MY LORD WHAT A MORNING

My Lord what a morning;
My Lord what a morning;
Oh, my Lord what a morning,
when the stars begin to fall.

You'll hear the trumpet sound
to wake the nations underground,
looking to my God s'right hand
when the stars begin to fall.

You'll hear the sinner cry.
to wake the nations underground,
looking to my God's right hand when
the stars begin to fall.

You'll hear the Christian shout
to wake the nations underground,
looking to my God's right hand
when the stars begin to fall.

Traditional Spiritual
Bruce Davidson, *Girls Dressed in their Sunday Best*, 1966
Bruce Davidson Collection, 'East 100th Street', St. Ann's Press

IF YOU SEE MY SAVIOR

I was standing by the bedside of a neighbor
Who was bound to cross Jordan's swelling tide
And I asked him if he would do me a favor
And kindly take this message to the other side

If you see my Savior, tell Him that you saw me
Ah, and when you saw me, I was on my way
When you reach that golden city think about me
And don't forget to tell the Savior what I said

Though you have to make this journey on without me
Oh, that's a debt that sooner or later must be paid
Well, you may see some old friends who may ask about me
Oh, tell them I am coming home someday

Thomas A. Dorsey, 1926
Jack Delany, *Portrait of an African American Boy*, 1941

OH SHENANDOAH

Oh, Shenandoah, I long to hear you
Away, you rolling river
Oh, Shenandoah, I long to hear you
Away, I'm bound away, cross the wide Missouri

Oh, Shenandoah, I love your daughter
Away, you rolling river
Oh, Shenandoah, I love your daughter
Away, I'm bound away, cross the wide Missouri

Oh, Shenandoah, I'm bound to leave you
Away, you rolling river
Oh, Shenandoah, I'm bound to leave you
Away, I'm bound away, cross the wide Missouri

Oh, Shenandoah, I long to see you
Away, you rolling river
Oh, Shenandoah, I long to see you
Away, I'm bound away, cross the wide Missouri

Traditional Spiritual
Mortimer Borne, *Alleyne*, c.1935-1943
Gift of the Works Projects Administration, New York, 1943
The Metropolitan Museum of New York

HONEY IN THE ROCK

O my brother, do you know the Savior,
Who is wondrous, kind, and true
He's the Rock of your salvation
There's honey in the Rock for you.

Oh, there's honey in the Rock, my brother;
There's honey in the Rock for you;
Leave your sins for the blood to cover;
There's honey in the Rock for you.

Have you tasted that the Lord is gracious.
So you walk in the way that's new
Have you drunk from the living fountain
There's honey in the Rock for you.

Then go out through the streets and byways,
Reach the Word to the many or few;
Say to every fallen brother,
There's honey in the Rock for you.

Frederick A. Graves, 1895
Harry Roseland, *Watching the Bluejay*, c.1900
Private Collection

LEANING ON EVERLASTING ARMS

What a fellowship, what a joy divine,
leaning on the everlasting arms;
what a blessedness, what a peace is mine,
leaning on the everlasting arms.

Leaning, leaning,
safe and secure from all alarms;
leaning, leaning,
leaning on the everlasting arms.

O how sweet to walk in this pilgrim way,
leaning on the everlasting arms;
O how bright the path grows from day to day,
leaning on the everlasting arms.

What have I to dread, what have I to fear,
leaning on the everlasting arms?
I have blessed peace with my Lord so near,
leaning on the everlasting arms.

Anthony J. Showalter, 1887
Photographer Unknown, 1922

EVERY TIME I FEEL THE SPIRIT

Every time I feel the Spirit
Moving in my heart, I will pray.

Yes, every time I feel the Spirit
Moving in my heart, I will pray.

Upon the mountain, when my Lord spoke,
Out of God's mouth came fire and smoke.

Looked all around me, it looked so fine, '
'Til I asked my Lord if all was mine.

Jordan River, chilly and cold,
It chills the body, but not the soul.

There is but one train upon this track;
It runs to heaven and then right back.

Traditional Spiritual
Photographer Unknown

AMAZING GRACE

Amazing grace, how sweet the sound
That saved a wretch like me!
I once was lost, but now am found;
Was blind, but now I see.

Through many dangers, toils and snares,
I have already come;
'Tis grace hath brought me safe thus far,
And grace will lead me home.

The Lord has promised good to me,
His Word my hope secures;
He will my Shield and portion be,
As long as life endures.

Yea, when this flesh and heart shall fail,
And mortal life shall cease,
I shall possess, within the veil,
A life of joy and peace.

The earth shall soon dissolve like snow,
The sun forbear to shine;

But God, who called me here below,
Will be forever mine.

When we've been there ten thousand years,
Bright shining as the sun,
We've no less days to sing God's praise

Than when we'd first begun.

John Newton, 1779
Photographer Unknown, *A Child Praying Before Lunch*, 1936

COME DOWN, ANGELS

Come down, Angels, a trouble the water.
Let God's saints come in.

I love to shout,
I love to sing
Let God's saints come in.

I love to praise my heavenly King,
Let God's saints come in.

I think I hear the Sinner say
Let God's saints come in.

My Savior taught me how to pray
Let God's saints come in.

Come down, Angels, trouble the water.
Let God's saints come in.

Down, down, down, down trouble the water,
Let God's saints come in.

Traditional Spiritual
Eudora Welty, *Baby Bluebird*, c.1930
Eudora Welty Collection,
Mississippi Department of Archives and History

PASS ME NOT,
O GENTLE SAVIOR

Pass me not, O gentle Savior;
hear my humble cry;
while on others thou art calling,
do not pass me by.

Savior, Savior,
hear my humble cry;
while on others thou art calling,
do not pass me by.

Let me at thy throne of mercy
find a sweet relief;
kneeling there in deep contrition,
help my unbelief.

Trusting only in thy merit,
would I seek thy face;
heal my wounded, broken spirit,
save me by thy grace.

Thou the spring of all my comfort,
more than life to me,
whom have I on earth beside thee?
Whom in heaven but thee?

Fanny Crosby, 1868
Photographer Unknown

Made in the USA
Columbia, SC
20 July 2021